SELECTED POEMS

THE MACMILLAN COMPANY
NEW YORK • CHICAGO
DALLAS • ATLANTA • SAN FRANCISCO
LONDON • MANILA

IN CANADA
BRETT-MACMILLAN LTD.
GALT, ONTARIO

SELECTED POEMS

FRANCIS GOLFFING

New York - The Macmillan Company - 1961

First Printing

"Interlude" appeared in *Hudson Review*, Summer, 1955.

"New Hampshire Eclogue" appeared in *Commentary*, June, 1959.

Other poems in this volume have previously appeared in *Briarcliff Quarterly*, *Epoch*, *Experiment*, *Folio*, *The Nation*, *Noonday*, *Partisan Review*, *Poetry*, *Quarterly Review of Literature*, *Sewanee Review*, *Voices*, *Wake*, and *Western Review*.

The Macmillan Company, New York
Brett-Macmillan Ltd., Galt, Ontario

Printed in the United States of America

Library of Congress catalog card number: 61-13992

THE ARROW OF SENSE

The Heart of the Park

The gardener trims the dead wood from the branches,
In the day's eclipse, abroad in a grove of willows.
His gloves, bark-spattered, tell the time is zero.

The sunlight trims the new leaves from the branches,
Sheen killing sheen, till each trunk ringed with children
Rises, a crape-wound widower, toward the zenith.

His gloves removed, in a swoon of the soft season,
The gardener goes and his shears cast no shadow.
Though trees have watched the sun decline from zenith
A child plays on till time is wrung to zero.
The shadows trim the light wood from the branches.

Contact: Variations on a Theme

Now jamb and lintel cease to be estranged
I view the eminent challenge from the air
Calmly.
    Let me distinguish what is left:
The untouched glove still tilted on the floor
And, churning in the dry chrysanthemums,
A casual draught which, heedless of the door,
Tells me the time of day.
        Nothing has changed.

Step on the leopard made into a rug
Or humbly go down on your knees to hug
His prone insidious head; profess
Touching the hide a tanner's knowingness:
Such conduct finds me fearful lest the flies
That spawn along the selvedge turn and scatter
And in the place of small inaccurate matter
Spots of the leopard start into my eyes.

My toes touched on a pebble
 Casual among rubble

And rolled it over the shovel
 That binds and divorces gravel

Down to the strand where boulders
 Rose from a mist of algae:

How little the stone went under!
 It shone bright in the water

Toward Asia

The standards glisten through the oleander;
The cohorts stiffen, ready to deploy.
A fine mist rises from Scamander.
Their faces hot with longing for Briseïs
Impatient heroes stamp the plain of Troy.

What husky angel, enemy of bustle,
Would keep such strenuous beauties from my view?
Let his eyes glower, his wings rustle:
The shreds of sleep still tasseling my forehead
I walk into that emerald-tinted blue.

An Old Lawyer Hallucinates

       I'm happy that this spring
I see my birds fly vertically up
And, circling round the battle monument,
Vanish into interstices of air
Before they drop as sheer as they ascended.
Through season after season have I watched
How they would perch on chimney or red roof,
Prompt at the slightest bidding of the breeze
To wheel and scatter westward, out of mind—
But not today, not in this happy spring.

       I'm happy that this spring
All cars have brand-new signals, all men cars
Who crowd the grounds where I have sat so long—
Too long perhaps and still not long enough
To see desire die and pulse grow faint.
My strong left hand clutching the field glasses
I wait for the last bird or plane to roar
Across my range of vision, distantly
And yet so clearly that the eye can shoot
And the heart bury it, this happy spring.

       I'm happy that this spring
Presiding at my tennis court once more
I see bright balls in motion, flying forth
At the bidding of such blithe antagonists
As I have summoned from our neighborhood.
Knowing this is a court of no appeal
Makes them, I warrant, keep their spirits up.
A game both gayer and more desperate
Was never yet conducted on man's lawn
Than that old game of mine, this happy spring.

       I'm happy that this spring
Tepid and blowing with irregular gusts,

Finds me propped in my garden chair, intact,
Save for the gangrene spreading through one thigh,
Which, being tended by my next of kin
With that same gentleness they've always shown
Towards every recent growth in father's garden
Will soon subside. Ah, gather round my knees
And glory in destruction, for I'm mortal
This spring, especially, this happy spring.

April, 1955

The Spot

The tingling in the loins,
The tinkling in the till,
Of what by day is Coins,
Of what by night is Will,

Distracts the neophyte,
And words the pickled sage
Has spelt but dare not write
Shudder against the page.

No matter where I turn
Or if I turn at all
I am made to discern
The foliage of the Fall,

The impenitent Spot,
And all the strength of art
Twisted into a knot
I cannot break apart . . .

What lightning from the blue
Will blast this mess of fears?
The poet's *je m'en fous*
Reverberates in my ears.

The Orchard: To a Friend

Maundering among trees that would disown
A knowledge vastly different from your own

And by the river where a sloping down
Conducts inferior reptiles up and down

You gloss the vegetation, and your tact
Presumes each detail of the scene intact,

Though some peripheral branches in the rear,
Charmed by your tenor, might be seen to rear

And the apple, sovereign orb of this vignette,
Adam, of your teeth shows the imprint yet.

A Dialogue

'It is my favourite season of the year
When fluid error manages to freeze
Within the gilded cadre of this glass
And, freezing, grows determinate and truth.
No longer gaze on the deserted air
But wonder at my formal aviary.'

Engross midwinter with experiments:
Humours will change, and over oblique roofs
Water will gaily splash onto your mirror
And spray will settle in your halcyon hair,
Deriding the barrette where white birds kiss.

Double and Single

Though I still draw the figure eight
With all the spirit it deserves
From him who was its votary
Before a slight shock in his nerves
Tilted the balance, slipped a weight
And made him doubt of symmetry:

I cannot, eager to repair
The module of your native hue
Ally it with another tense
But must forsake the form I knew
And from your blanched fantastic hair
Distil a fine impermanence.

The Sibyl

We were betrothed in the falling year
With water darting over the rocks
And a cedar branch whipping the bleak air.

It was the time of medallions
Prodigal of locks and looks
In this swiftest of seasons,

And what the rooks cried and did not cry
Fell on our ears, enchanted
With the discordant minstrelsy

Moving the heath, and the taunting
Twilight hard against our skins
Till the lemon streak fainted.

We were betrothed in the crumbling brake
With the desert wind close on the sun's
Heels, and rising from the dry creek

Fossils of love, the never perjured
Voice of the sibyl, the hushed amens,
Responding, of the calm dead.

Artemis

Whom the tall wood let in
—Wading in the trefoil
And distilling a sin
From the sanctity of the soil—

Feels his brassart estranged,
Under the greaves no shin
And tuille and tasses changed
To a target of tin.

While the feathered arrow whirs
Indeflectible through firs
I, stronger than my risk

Till susurrations cease,
Wait within the glittering disk
The truculence of your peace

Dry Gold

Inside my threaded ear
I hear what is not here
Or there or anywhere:
A grinding as of saws
Through boards of burnished time;
A scratching as of paws
Upon a gilded stair
They never learnt to climb.

Inside my tunnelled eye
I see Greek laurel lie
Unfathomable, cold:
See, yes, and hate to see
Its execrable sheen
Shamming eternity
With gloss too densely green
And long abolished gold.

Inside my deep-drilled mouth
I dread the taste of drouth
Which summer's penury
Has processed for my need
From goldenrod, bright hay.
You cry the mind is free,
The years, the year, still young . . . ?
Across my palate speed
Moist scatterings of May:
They barely wet my tongue.

July, 1955

14

A Young Woman Washing Clothes in Her Back Yard

When laved upon the line your lingerie
Is ravished in a body by the sun
  I stand and marvel at the spectre:
Whom Phoebus harries is no prey for me
Nor dare I rise in arms as her protector.
The sheer and bleaching carnage must go on.

Your public self, meanwhile, need ask no truce;
Laundress, the gods shall spare you, tub and all,
  As they have spared much readier wenches.
Ah mortal made for mortals to seduce,
How soon after the leaves that hide these branches
The mercury of your soul will start to fall!

October

Fast lorries on the road,
  O love it is not this
But what the hooded mind
Lately accompanies:

The green leaf and the red
Swept up by the same gust
And risen where they rose
In mimicry of dust

Such swarming embassies
As fall will organize
Moving toward flocks of snow
From half-remembered flies.

How slender in its hearse
The year, how briefly borne,
How light these ministrants
Who vanish as they mourn,

How ready on that grave
The couple in whose kiss
The lorries brake and scream:
  O love it is not this

Poem

Don't ask me to digress
on the frothy surface of your mattress
or on the velvet shell
whose convolutions obscure the marvel.
Let the patient orchid
which I've cut to wither in love's parlor
reiterate the flor-
al beauty of wet cheek and fluttering lid.

Nightfall

They sprawl against the window, amateurs,
Peeling the onion, telling you at length
In verse what none would hear in prose.
                                    The prose
Of evening potent in the window frame
Slowly obliterates the room and blurs
Those light-points sharp as needles in your eyes,
While, treacherously tame
Yet unpersuaded, energy of thighs
Gathers between your knickers and your hose.

Drinking at Dusk

Never from any pitcher poured that fluid
Not global but enough for some to drown in:
Out of the ground and streaming through the woodland
One peace invades another with its cohorts.

This tumbler here holds what is left of opal
And as I down the day for brief assurance
New knowledge quickens round each fiery globule.

Knowledge too raw? too burnt?
                                All hues gone umber,
My meadow moves its shadow up the mountain.
The giant mountain drinks it absolutely.

August, 1955

An Expostulation

The glassy stare, the eyelashes that bat
To shutter gaze from gaze and view from view,
The spied-on spies, the vacant habitat
Of what was you-in-me or me-in-you

Compel me quite, your erstwhile governor,
To fixed convergence on an inward beam,
While images once active at my door
Mimic the motions of your disesteem

I've roused no rabble in the public square
But rather stopped marauders who would fare
Upon the road from brow to occiput:

Even as the iris' quick indictment tries
To rout a legion swarming in the skies
I shift from thought to thought and foot to foot

Glimpses in the Rear-View Mirror:
Pool and Quarry

Looking into the glass I see
The symmetry distorted of your face,
Or from a casual fault in my perception
Or from a fine ingenerate flaw
Or from a flaw yet finer in the mirror.
Ah do not start at such discountenance,
Knowing the slight pretensions of your judge
Content to drive along the edge of pleasure:
I'm but an image cast up by your dream;
Across my chest heraldically I bear
The curious blots and scratches of a pen
That wrote, rebelled, and wrote. Placed thus beside you
I'm to your text a running commentary
As ripples to the figure of a quarry.
The pond will soon freeze over, you remark,
But in the cold December light of evening
Those marble blocks are rosier than at dawn.

Cradle Song for a Young Sailor

Lie in a coma, lie and re-enact
Rising desire and the consummate fact
   Of your first metamorphosis.
Under the nurse's anesthetic kiss
Forget the wars of Toonerville and this.

My love would say, 'Tails you lose, heads I win.'
Drowned in the ocean of his medicine
   Let that perverse eidolon, Love,
Inflame your senses, while the tide above
Tosses the surgeon's antiseptic glove.

Dialogue at Midnight

'Threatened by too much shade,
The adulterous bed unmade,
How can I view my trust
Squarely, as soon I must?'

Your trust will be undone
By a ray of the sun,
By a stroke of the clock.

'Since clocks are fast or slow,
How shall the victim know
When her trust is betrayed?'

Skeptical child, sleep on:
I'll be the cock and crow.

An Exhortation

Take the wheel of your racing-car,
   Mover, yourself unmoved
Though Aeolus bid his winds rise from the cave
   And pile storm-clouds, bar on bar,
Against a progress he has not approved.

Pay no heed to this lord's decree
   Who even as you steer
Through the first layer of rack will be your slave,
   Changed by the fierce sympathy
That, passing across vapor, leaves it clear.

A Vanished House

Deep in the intrepid glamour
     Cosseted and contained
I moved, though enemy to my kind,
Velvety against silver.
     Everything shone, from floor to mantel
And I, feeding among the lilies:
   Hostesses, your perfection was
More than a matter of doilies.

The smoke, violent, from your chimney
     Soon abandoned the walls
In a silence of whippoorwills
As you poured your hearts' strong tea.
     Over the sumac hedge, past the maples
To the red horse-barn's fern-locked challenge
   Rose at once familiar and strange
The odor of your examples.

Only rarely what seemed a nimbus
     Round the admirable sun
Would release a shower and be gone.
Elegies, no, nor dithyrambs
     Become that trim, permanent season
Drawn about me with Watteau's contour;
   Now a whirl of leaves has set in;
Now I turn and it is winter.

Interlude

And so I reached the well.
The waters rose and fell
Even as was their wont
When, priestess, by the font

Your tawny eyes, intent,
Watched for the sacrament
Capable to amaze
This moist autumnal haze.

With Julian under sod
The unforgiving god
Now scorns of his own will
To crown a vacant hill

Nor, in the desperate night,
Shall the fond acolyte
Poised on the fountain's rim
Spy any sign of him.

Unless, beside these walls,
One afternoon there falls
His gaze on the long rest
Of gods unmanifest:

Immovable and stark
Protectors of the park
The Tuscan lions keep
Smiling as they sleep.

AIRS FOR THE MIND

Air

Voices? but no one spoke:
Only the crystal joke
Of a snowy morning.

Only a sunbeam split
Into its white and yolk,
Conversing with the click
Of the frost on the pane.

Weather, don't move the vane
While I listen: a tick
As of clocks; while I sit
Sharpening my own wit.

Voices? but no one spoke:
Only the crystal joke
Of a snowy morning.

Air of the Roadmender

Bright resident of day!
The road is ready.
                    Stay.

I've watched the sturdy burro
Falter up the hill,
The tinker with his barrow
Glide tawnily toward hell

And through no fault of either,
Bright resident of day!
I'd be the latter, rather.
The road is ready.
                    Stay.

Lines to a Man
Whose Marriage Went
Suddenly to Pieces

You fancied
your marriage
both mobile
and stable:
two horses,
a carriage,
a kitchen,
a table

While you drum
with your cutler-
y tunes
on your plate,
hear the voice
of the butler:
'Sir, lunch will be
'late

'The gravy,
'the scalloped
'potatoes,
'the tray
'have mounted
'the horses
'and galloped
'away

Before the Bench

Testily, testily,
Testily I shoot glances.

When the scaffolding broke
I remembered my schema:
The ciphers were crimson,
The rubrics alive.
I awoke in the dark
To a hidden aroma
And the garden resounded
With the hum of the hive.

But here comes the valet
(I'd forgotten the schemer)
His habit is scarlet,
His envelope glossy.
How dim in the distance
The sound of remission!
The scaffold goes up.
The court is in session.

Testily, testily,
Testily I shoot glances.

Song of the Cook at a Public Fête

Two or three dancers are standing in the arena
Brooding on the significancy of things,
Several Magi, each in a special tiara,
Keep the kitchen supplied with their offerings.

One, it is true, while I stirred this feast of the palate
Licked the side of the dish to confirm its fault . . .
Friend, you need not have choked as you did when you swal-
  lowed:
What I put in the sauce was a mere suspicion of salt.

The Cross

The sound of cavalry
Comes ebbing on the wind.
Wind is my torturer:
Impatient to abet
Driving rain and sleet;
Patient to join with snow
In timbering my cross.
I'm leeched with snails of wet
Which will freeze when the snows
Start from the mountain tops
Down every glen and coomb.
The horsemen and their drums
Are silenced by the wind:
Who goes there? No one goes
As from my Calvary,
Ice-ridden, I descend.

A Cold February Morning

While the log hisses, I'm not done.
Why should this day, chameleon,
Green-spot the frost-bloom on our windows?
Your knitting needles as they ply
Draw fuel from my fantasy:
Let martyrs shout for tongs and bellows;
Beware that sudden strain of Liszt
Which tempts you, tongueless, to be kissed,
Me, witless, to improve on Adam
By being tree and snake in one . . .
With praise of lamblike virtue, madam,
While the log hisses I'm not done.

HEART OF CONTRADICTION

Three Passages from The Long Dispute

The ram now with the winding of his horn
Unwinds me from a slumber scarcely stirred
By breath, and I am summoned to be born,

And catapulted hard among the herd
Begin my circuit of this city lot
With other heaven-plunged beasts and disinterred

And crop such meagre grass as they forgot.
Hard were the living in these places, yes,
Where favorable Phoebus never shot

His beam but for your care, O shepherdess,
Who manage knotted stick and water-pail
Each in its turn with exquisite address;

Nor, should a tyro (like this latest) fail
Of strict performance—loiter or lament
Tomorrow's shearing—will the least detail

Whether of comfort or due punishment
Change; nor yet one proprietary glance
Or hint of censure passionately spent

Break from your eyes so long as herds advance
Even as they must: for Justice willed it so
Who cannot palter with the clowns of chance,
Clad in the green of mercy though they go.

II

Such calm disturbs my neighbor: among men
A leader; whom the Heaven of Real Estate
Could not, they say, endorse as citizen

Till he was dropped; in business and debate
Sharp as a razor once, but fair withal;
Now grown cantankerous, a sorry mate,

Constantly harping on his double fall.
This neighbor, then, one evening as the dusk
Had quite absorbed our gracious keeper's call

Lurched towards me with a grin; some long-stemmed husk
—Last remnant of his miserable meal—
Stuck to his teeth, half tentacle half tusk,

Teasing the dark. "I wish I could conceal,"
He said, "the chronic jaundice of my mood.
I understand how younger tups must feel

And, though your manner certainly is rude,
Grant every jibe a modicum of truth.
But what of *her?* through whose ineptitude

I've come to be that ram 'long in the tooth,'
'Dyed in the wool,' that 'hunk of mutton'—tags
As accurate as they are cruel and uncouth?

I'd rather have a shepherdess who nags,
Some silly crosspatch or fierce termagant,
Nay, live in bondage to the Queen of Hags,

Than put up with the equitable cant
Of this our mistress." Here he stopped and threw
One look at me, then said: "I know this rant

Will hardly serve to raise me in your view.
And yet my claim is simple: creature's right
To score an order patently askew;

Speak out, that is; not preach or proselyte:
We're sheep, not pastors." "Delicate of hoof,"
I cried, "who toe the line dividing spite

From rank rebellion: favor me with proof
For any proposition but the last."
"Surely," he said, "you've heard of warp and woof,

Pestle and mortar, and how each is cast
In a secure yet fragmentary role.
Dreary dependence makes their union fast

But, luckily, a pestle has no soul.
Nor would I claim the merchant's balance does
Which yet some view as being, on the whole,

To our great creature world analogous:
For even as scales swinging in free accord
Do we depend on others, they on us;

And as a scale-pan momently outsoared
By its companion shall climb up in turn
Towards briefest triumph: so shall either lord

Or vassal, in a trade of stations, learn
That height and depth do not exist as such.
Here, then, you have the gist of my concern:

Logic and I have long been out of touch."
The ram sighed and fell silent. Suddenly
She whose dim orb had never moved me much

These many years, rose in her majesty
And sweeping past some desperate tenements
Which, on one side, define our boundary

Began to shed her spectral influence.
So will a queen hearing the vulgar rush
To a rude feast near her own residence

Banish such trivial anger as might flush
A lesser lady's cheek and wait, aloof,
For the first hint of comfortable hush

To speed her on the scene, with no reproof
Other than her high presence. "Still," I mused,
"If streaks of silver patterning a roof

Were punishment: why, being so purely used,
Should sinner, when sin beckons him, resist?"
And all at once the moon seemed interfused

With a corona, like a ring of mist,
And turning towards the ground I seemed to catch
The impassive sneer of my antagonist

Huddled, disconsolate, on his seedy patch
As one too long familiar with the tune
To spell its regular measures in a thatch.

My glad Arcadia lapsed into a swoon
As Luna hid, and in her place the glow
Of some electric substitute for moon

Flooded, against a set by Chirico,
The waxen shape of bloody Bonaparte,
His baton buried in a drift of snow.

The vision faded. But what mortal art
Could so induce on a mere mortal's sight
Damage made permanent? so unhinge his heart

That, for a second, he would expedite
General ruin, crush distinctions flat
And make the ram seem colorably right?

Who now resumed his discourse where he sat:
"The indifferent butcher thinking he employs
This thingamabob to weigh his gristle and fat

Burns incense in your chapel, O Equipoise.
Hail, goddess! long immortalized in paint
And printed word; creator of blind noise;

Sacred to sheep albeit the patron saint
Of butchers; whom this crooked world obeys
Because you're dead; as dead, with all your quaint

Accoutrements as the meat the butcher weighs
In those distinguished scales of yours, except
That the dumb animal's ghost still bleats, lows, neighs

Close to its slayer's ears, while you have kept
Intact your inexistence since the days
When dawn was pure, and all creation slept."

III

How strange that I should dream (though no more strange
Than all dreams are we creatures entertain)
Our mistress had been subject to such change

That I, most fervent of her ample train,
Was moved to falter and desert the team
Which yet continued faithful under strain . . .

The dawn broke yellow in my midnight dream;
My ears were struck by a dramatic sound
That made us issue in a sluggish stream

Beyond the pasture onto open ground,
While she with ready switch and scathing words
Scorned the sweet law to which we were all bound.

Stumbling through bracken, like untutored herds,
Or against rocks, we'd suddenly take fright
When the clear sun seemed darkened by great birds:

Bad augury! for towards the fall of night
The ocean rose, gigantic, flecked with green
And dirty grey shading to dirty white.

43

She, spruce deviser of this sloppy scene,
Now crossed herself, as was her privilege,
Then watched file past the victims of her spleen

Till we had come close to the water's edge.
"Keep on!" she cried, and forward all sheep went
But me, who halted at the final ledge

And with one hoof assayed the element,
Then turned, as one who knowing he has tried
And failed will turn to meet his punishment,

And met her far-off eyes which justified
Each tiniest ripple on this sea of snot
While the bell-wether gamboled on the tide,
His flock still following, though I could not.

A Scene of Crime

For Stanley Kunitz

I saw the strapped assassin clasp
Each side of the electric chair
And scream a curse for sole reply
Across the unanswerable air.

> *With what abandon before dawn*
> *His child-ghost fluttered up the stair*
> *And to the very rafters filled*
> *Man's attic with a peccant air!*

Into the current of that curse
I heard your wretched trumpets blare,
O Angels who on Judgment Day
Shall blast each peaceful sleeper's ear.

> *The widow ravished in her bath,*
> *The drab he mangled at the fair*
> *Are now mere motions of his voice*
> *That circle on the empty air,*

And what those village Strephons railed
To nerve man's executioner
Turns to a rattle in the throat
Dying upon its sister, air.

> *We have no shepherds to entreat;*
> *Their Lalages have risen far*
> *Above the towers of our still*
> *More extraordinary air.*

Green banners blister in the sun,
The crowd disbands without a prayer,
And who's left to evangelize
But this sharp apostolic air?

45

Supplication to Master Thomas, for Abatement

When the dread silence tapped by every word
Breaks out in coruscations to relumine
The original cue and countenance of the Lord,
Gracious my master, condescend to seat
On tips of letters minims of acumen
Or train a trick of lighting on their feet!

Fourteen Epigrams

I

Who draw the distant closer as they peer
Upon the farthest edge of thought, appear
To carve intentions singly, like a frieze:
Perspective has no power over these.

II

The Coppice

Endurance has no meaning in this grove
Nor pride that scorns velleities of love:
Both what I would not bear and what I bore
Are needles littering the pine-wood floor.

III

Like scattered nebulae my notions rise,
Their general scope no lesser than the sky's,
Their destinies ungoverned by the sun,
Toward the dim reaches of oblivion.

IV

Sleeping, I am awake; awake, asleep
Save for those spurious vigils which I keep
When the long daylight pausing on the broad
Canal finds me, somnambulist, abroad.

V

Point of Death: In Memory of a Cat

Shut eyes and shut book,
For the mind scarce forgets
That hot day at the vet's
When I sent a long last look

Through the bars of your cage:
There you lay, out of the pets'
And poet's realm, your own image.
The ground where I stood shook.

VI

On Prescience

Smitten with too much foresight, I resigned
All but the scrupulous silence of the mind.
Myself a ghost I now move among ghosts
And (prophets rarely trouble with detail)
Hear no more topical gibes or cocktail boasts
But Hector swagger and Thersites rail.

VII

To a Recent Believer

What if, through uplands, tongues of Pentecost
Burst each successive lock on fields and ditches?
Fafnir still holds in escrow those new riches;
Your nether valleys shiver in his frost.

VIII

To Prince, Writer of Satires

All would be well were you but mean enough.
You do not ply your rogue's trade roguishly
But as a child of diffident probity
Might learn to steal to make his fibre tough.

IX

To a Friend, on Evil Redounding to Good

Stick up for goodness but, for goodness' sake,
Give hornets leave to sting you by mistake.

X

To Dr. Maclure, on His Rehearsing of Symptoms

Great are my pains and greater still, I'm sure,
The pains I should be destined to endure
But for your coming. Now you've come, Maclure,
Skip the disease: I'm ready for the cure.

XI

Howard, this blade of stricken grass
Is what you were, what I was,
What you will be, and I, and all
Kindred, man or animal,
Who now in our green lust abound
On a more ravenous ground.

XII

*The Castaway Poets to the Great Grocer,
Prince of This World*

Provider of canned seaweed, comfort us,
Champion of self-help, don't withdraw your help
When, shipwrecked, through the beard of Proteus
We drift who are less usable than kelp.

XIII

*A Museum Guide Explains to the
Visitors a Classical Scene*

Beside the idol flashing in the sun
You see, with no uncertain pencil drawn,
The man of reason, looking like a fool
Among haruspices consulting stool.

49

XIV

Speech from a Baroque Play

Cease to examine with such care, my brother,
Each bloody spot upon the bedroom wall.
This life is all you have; there comes no other;
Let it not fade into your funeral.

Reflection at Daybreak

A mote's weight on a screw
Makes me stop or go, makes me stall or do;
    I continue to die and live.
Above the trees the gold is sensitive
    While I turn on my doubt,
Impelled by wheels within wheels and without,
    Ready for the faint trem-
or that will seize an oakleaf and my stem,
    For the sting of surprise
If I should pause or run counterclockwise.

L'Esprit Sérieux

> The 'serious' man . . . agrees to the
> identification of himself with an
> arbitrary function which society has
> bestowed.

Identify me with my function, see
In me the headwaiter and nothing more.
My destiny is bounded by this floor.

My footfall echoing through the corridors
Gives me no guilty start; my fancy moves,
Domestic, in unalterable grooves.

My colleagues either relish the absurd
Or have their avocations, hunt and fish:
To be the headwaiter is all I wish.

When in my dreams I re-enact my life
Each act shows such propriety and sense
As though I'd never heard of *Existenz*.

Yet several colleagues on the upper floor
Hope to infect me with their *idées fixes;*
They say I'll learn—I'm only fifty-six—;

They say instead of dreaming of the smooth
Parquet on which I like a dancer glide,
I'll dream of Kafka and of suicide,

Of tips I hoarded, of serviettes I soiled,
Of guests I snubbed, of girls I coveted
Pretending to lie primly on my bed,

Of gnawing *Sorge*, of the dizzy Naught,
Of a weird rival in seniority
Who snatching at my function will snatch me . . .

The Answer

If Jack and John are still the same, you ask?
Children, they faced each other from their beds
To recognize a likeness in their features,
Authentic but too brief.
                              Then, growing up
And desperate to distinguish each from each
They drove their stakes beside their flower beds,
One red, one green, and crouching junglewise
Fixed one another in an orange stare
That would not fade upon the fading light.
Nor shall the eddying years unfreeze their postures:
The stakes still placed beside the beds, the men
Still placed beside the stakes, there is maintained
Inexorable through the phantom garden
A sense of limits and of hostile peace
Against the wind with rising difficulty.

To a Snail

Your sensitive exposed flesh as you pass
Might well disarm those deputies of doom
  Who with tensed claw and beak agape
Spread menace from the air or through the grass.
But as a window hardens into glass
And so destroys the mullion whose design
Was its own tegument, you raise a shape
Of brittlest fibre upon fluid line,
Making your progress, like our human, crass
And death expected in that living room.

A Ballad of Reckoning

I tried to square my account
With a clerk's indelible pencil
On a squared immaculate sheet.
Unsettled, I strained to settle
A most confounding account.
My mind reduced to a stencil,
My lips compressed in a mould
I strove in vain to account
For the shifts of insensible gold.

I tried to close my account
Of plot and shelter and raiment,
Of tea and kettle and heat.
That day I was on my mettle
And trifles of no account
I marked for credit or payment:
Yet some sprite eluded me still
And I left him out of account
Though I checked each voucher and bill.

Prince, my figures are neat;
Your auditors praise my fine fettle:
But the tea's grown cold in the kettle;
The kettle upsets my account.

Sonnet

(After the German of R. A. Schröder)

Were you to wake me with your fires from
The profound gloom of solitary thought,
Your flaming hand outstretched for me to come,
Routing with flashes the soul's dream of Naught,

Were you to seek me from your battlements,
My stormy sovereign, with each several wind,
That secret chasm you should never find
Where I took shelter, warily, long since.

What use is it to try your look on me
Or your commandments from the castled skies?
I've slunk away from any destiny
That would enrol me, and to paralyze

Each striking arm, dived into the dull flood.
What use, lord of the living? I am shrewd.

Two Sonnets After Francisco Quevedo

I

Of this our mortal life the several years
Sweep onward, mocking at our youthful ardors,
Courage of iron and even the cold marble
Which against Time its eminent hardness rears.

I had not yet learnt to walk when my feet strayed
Into the wake of death and that is where
I steer my obscure life likewise: slight river
To be drunk, black ocean, by your towering waves.

Every new moment is another step
I'm taking to my cost on this voyage
For whether I sleep or wake I cannot stop.

Death is a brief, final and bitter breathing,
But if that overmastering heritage
Is law not punishment, why am I grieving?

II

In the deepest recesses of my soul
The hurt dwells, but how steadily it feeds
On my existence as the brand proceeds
Along the tender marrow, wasting all!

Hydroptic ardor still harasses one
Long turned to loving insubstantial ash,
The smoking remnant, lying in dead hush,
Of, beauty, your divine conflagration.

Men I avoid and flee from the sun's light;
In a loud voice I intone my lament
Which the wind carries to the supine ocean.

My sighs are vocables of a dark chant,
My soul is swamped and bitter with confusion,
My heart the unbounded seignory of fright.

Savor

My father sired me as best he could
While condiments were coursing in his blood,
Thinking it subtle practice to commit
To a tough and sanguine world a ghost of wit.
Now, to repair my pungent maker's fault,
I spit up with each word a grain of salt.

A Forward Spring

Mind moving at will
Though never far away,
Slip through the knot of May
    Back into April;
There make my eyes unsee,
Unsay their being glad:
The torsion in the tree
Was not yet the dryad.

September Sonnet

Spring caught me in its drift of sun-and-shade
Speculating about profit and loss,
Whether to keep my slender stake or toss
It on the table where the game is played.
Suppose I invest the past: should it be made
Over and given a new hem and gloss
Or left without lustre, its edges frayed,
Not even an apposite motto stitched across?

Summer's dazzlement teased my curtained eyes
Into vision. Slumped on a bed of ferns
I watched the termites forage for supplies.
Now that clear autumn in the foliage burns
I pray, distraught, that it may cauterize
My fallacy of predictable returns.

To Vincent: Of Truth

The truth of which you boast
Is breathed as shimmering air, then lost
To sister currents waiting to grow stale.
The truth which I inhale
Thus without damage to my system wrongs,
Vincent, some finer organ: I am not all lungs

Like him who shouting, 'Quick,
The iron to brand this maverick!'
Would stamp the brute for barter. Even so
Stamp each truth; have them know
Who trade with you that they are like to get
No vain gold of the air but sterling counterfeit.

To a Friend Who Found It Difficult to Write

When dry as grasshoppers your voice
Batters against your throat, let be.
Step to the window while it gives
On to the world's sweet average,

While all around nor yet too late
The slopes, the shaded lanes, the draws
Whisper enjoin commemorate
Varied intentions of terrain:

To watch a clean perspective scheme,
A web of lines coordinate
Knit with the circle and the swoop,
The lonely orbit of a bird,

And spreading through the valley floor
A holding on, a letting go,
Till between stress and counterstress
The restless eye is canceled out,
The throat retrieves its level tone.

I see a tree across a road.
I see a road across a ridge.
The hawk entranced with what is there
Consumes and is consumed by air.

The Tomb of Stéphane Mallarmé

Fled from the spot of Balder's burial
—Rime on the blade and torpid river course—
He, suitor to the Saxon clock, the all
But inaudible trickle of the source

Found fixity of candles where in rows
Desire freezes toward the patterned gloom
Of curtains ever ready to disclose
An apparition waiting for its womb.

Not the elixirs dreaming on the sill
Nor what the priestess hints of vertigo
Can tempt him, nodding in his chair, the mage

Of one more motion who at moonrise will
With the pen's downward stroke across the page
Descend into his own and lasting snow.

The Manikin

'If fairs must be, let them be fair not foul.
Erect, I'll shake those beetles from my brow:
Not all night-birds attend Minerva's owl.'

But the dank booth commands you to the spot
Behind the target. At each random shot
That hits Time's bull's-eye you jump out and bow.

Suggestions for Awards

It's time to give the engineer his medal
Whose train, now on a siding, ran on schedule,

And one to the captain who with macabre
Skill brought his ship and his corpse into harbor.

All proved technicians, whether prone or upright,
Have earned these disks of silver, which turn coppery

When the sun, active witness of glad tidings,
Lights up the terminus and the tall dry dock.

The Tongue: To Barbara

Pucker my mouth with alum till the taste
Of sweetmeat graces languish on the tongue:
Astringent I shall love you, for too long
Have I been feeding on the candied waste
That makes the palate of bright men unchaste.

Bright careless men have taught my tongue to sin
And then do penance upon sugar-spikes
As in a bell the waggish clapper strikes
Idly against its tegument of tin:
Shatter the mould and bid the tongue begin

Its term of continence that the strong alloy
Which you will furnish find its tip and heel
Equal in temper to whatever peal
May wait release; or, if I balk, destroy
As one more mockery my unborn joy.

Ode to the Memory of P. W. W., Painter

Muse, I would make a collage
Of the friend I have known and that far Tennessee where his life
Was both moulded and marred; would recover the attic
Where his heart first conceived a foreseeable joy
And the small mansard window from which he gazed on the pad-
    dock,
Spiritual and abstract, a St. Francis of birds.

But how could he thrive in this paddock
Heavy with horse dung, amid that gray stubble which birds
Largely disdain? His eyes, slanting, begot a collage
On the innocent ground, then fled to adventure a life
Where the long-handled brush impeccably kept in the attic
Would breathe onto each canvas a moment of joy.

O the child's fierce secret joy
As he tore the posts and rode through the breach in the paddock
Past the startled snake under the rock, the nesting bird,
While overhead the clouds composed a collage,
Wind-lashed, with such incongruous scraps of life
As shall not ever, he vows, re-litter his attic.

Yet what was his salt if not Attic,
Seasoning ever so little those meat-scraps which life
Leaves on our platter? I dream of his latest collage
Where wing of angel lies close against gizzard of bird
—Christ *in extremis* perhaps—, where the lord of the paddock
Shreds into sections the queasiest taste can enjoy.

Paul, even so: in this life
Could you be wholly at ease with the head in the attic
Leering from over your bedstead? No fountain of joy
Save for himself, your wire-drawn idol: collage
Of the Nazarene and Narcissus; svelte, mischievous bird
Ready to pounce on its prey in the sun-drenched paddock.

For you are back where the birds
Feed to be fed on; that bloody circle your joy
Overpassed for a spell; the unspeakable paddock
Out of mind's reach maybe yet forever watched from the attic
By the wild saviour you wrought and those knife-edged squares
    of collage
Which as they seamlessly closed had stripped you of life.

Rest in joy, sweet androgynous life, composed as your boldest
    collage,
While like mares in the paddock your sisters rage through the
    attic
Entranced with those pieces of truth they peck at like birds.

March, 1957
Berlin/Rome

The Arizona Desert, Filmed

The sky bears heavily down upon this ochre
Met by the upward thrust of carcases,
Incredible, last threat of mastodons
Whom sand has ravished, wishing them eternal.

> Here, if you can withstand that savage friction,
> Build yet another home; another Lawrence,
> Learn to distinguish lunar glaze from neon,
> Insatiate hope from credence, in your fiction;
> Weather the storm blown over in an aeon
> Finally to face time again, and action:
> The doe that, racing past you on the screen,
> Flexes her legs too lightly at the knee-joints:

Incredible along the crest of sierras
Travels a shape so fragile in construction.

January, 1957

New Hampshire Eclogue

I watched rude farmers toiling east of Keene:
One farmer's engine coming on a corpse
Ground through the bones, moved on, and no harm done—
No harm but to the gossamer-thin wraith
Winding its way toward distant Golgotha.
The unredeemed are strewn across the world,
Clipped in this torment sleek as a machine,
Their brave skulls used for playing skittles now
By jaunty seminarians after dark.
But some men's minds cannot too well digest
The word made flesh still writhing on its rack,
The raw bog sucking down indifferently
Sheriff and murdered man and murderer:
But, green-eyed sorceress peering from each tree
To see your bronze bees storming round their hive,
I keep your image in my pupil fixed
For yours, of all states, is the blessedest
Who driving all things draw them to yourself:
The great browned plane-leaves flapping in a gale
That comes from nowhere, or all sides at once,
Acknowledge you as motive, and I stare
At your blind Pythian will that portions out
To the dim fire-fly apprehending space
Its magic scope; or in deep woods allows
Brief fabulous dominion to the frog,
Or me to find enchanted in his tank
One tiny turtle worshipping the sun.

The Higher Empiricism

The reputed need for a 'myth'
disappears. The empirical world
is discovered to provide sufficient
'meaning,' adequate objects of desire.
ROBERT MOTHERWELL

O Visionary who adjust your lens
Till it is focused on a wheel of fire,
What spotless lover would you find in space?
Let wisdom guide you to the market place,
There to be broken on the wheel of sense
And burnt by adequate objects of desire.